CONNOTATIONS

Connotations

Poems by
MAURICE KENNY

WHITE PINE PRESS / BUFFALO, NEW YORK

Grateful appreciation to the journals and publications where the following poems first appeared or are forthcoming, occasionally in different form: *House Organ, Mobus Magazine, North Country Magazine, The Saranac Review,* and *Studies in American Indian Literature.* Several of these poems appeared in *The Mama Poems* (White Pine Press, 1984) and *Carving Hawk* (White Pine Press, 2002).

Publication of this book was made possible, in part, by a grant from the National Endowment for the Arts, which believes that a great nation deserves great art, and with public funds from the New York State Council on the Arts, a State Agency.

State of the Arts

First Edition.

Printed and bound in the United States of America.

Cover: Mike Kabotie (Hopi), "The Trickster's Laugh." Acrylic on canvas, 22 inches by 30 inches. Used by permission of the artist.

ISBN: 978-1-893996-96-0

Library of Congress Control Number: 2008921648

White Pine Press
P.O. Box 236
Buffalo, New York 14201
www.whitepine.org

In memory of

David Fisher...who cared
Fred Hoch...who painted
my good friend Barbara Cameron,
Lorne Simon...who was to be a strong writer
John B. Johnson...who helped publish my first book
and the beautiful Diane Burns.

All were friends

With thanks to

Eleanor, Nina and Ruth
Diane and Tim
George and Rochelle Owens Economou
Tony Tyler, Alan Steinberg, Rick Henry,
Anne Malone and Paul Saint-Armand, Susan Stebbins,
Cheryl Culotta and John Radigan
Sarah Iselin and Frank Parman,
Rob, Ross, Adam P., Adam L., Allison, Wil J.,
Silpa, Ben and Charlotte.

Who are friends

AUTHOR'S NOTES

I am behooved to drop a handful of words to thank my editor, Elaine LaMattina, for her creative skills and her astute abilities in editing this collection. She has mysteriously managed to compress two differing books of poetry and meld them together with ideas I had not considered.

Little did Ms. LaMattina guess that years back when in high school I dabbled in oil painting without success. However my father decided I could develop into a fine painter and earn a living, as I should never be successful in managing his gasoline station business, nor his restaurant, let alone become a high school teacher or football great. He actually wanted me to enter an art school. My thought was that was pure foolishnes as I would never make it there either. He held much less belief in my pen than in my brush, and considered me too shy to become a writer: he mistakenly believed I wished to become a newspaper journalist. He was right: I had no "nose" for news. I obviously wound up a college professor and poet.

In addition to the friends mentioned on the dedication page, I must thank Wil Johnson, Devin Rice, and Charlotte Aldrich for serving me for years at SUNY Potsdam as my work-study students. They did much more than just answer my telephone. I need also to mention Gen Salarno; my typist C.C. Martin; my colleagues Tony Boyle for years of morning coffee and Mark and Cynthia Coleman for extraordinary dinners. These wonderful students suffered under my smiles and my rage: Beth Hamilton, Chris Pierce, Jon Foote, Even Kelly, Mike Nichols, Rob Morris, Matt Graber, and Evan Mills. I grateful to Dan Hardy for the guitar music, Colin DeHond for his naughty lyrics, and Ryan Bradley, who drove us to Oxford, Mississippi, for the William Faulkner conference with Adam Lang. Thanks, too, to my hundreds of other students, especially Chad Sweeney, Dan Bodah, Katie Smith, and, naturally, Dean.

An extra thanks to my co-tea-drinkers, Silpa and Ben.

CONTENTS

CONNOTATIONS

Connotations

a line across stretched canvas
diagonal
      blue
          or
            green
                green
                    or
                      blue
similar to a warrior's paint
across the brow, down his cheek
x-ed on his chest
or rearing up from his horse's rump

a line painted diagonally
on a clean canvas
      red
        yellow
            yellow
                red
what real difference does it make
does it change Andrew's death
reinvent happiness
or does it remain the abstraction
      that death and happiness are
      purple splotch
painted a dead columbine, a dried mushroom
a sleeping panther
      tawny

PART I
LINES ON CANVAS

The job of the artist is always to deepen the mystery.
—Sir Francis Bacon

FRANCIS BACON

Slaughtered beef
hangs from a hook
raw and bloody
enough
to make a lion
eat bananas and grains

is this what you were
painting

nothing so simple
I'd suppose

but raw and bloody
slaughtered
an interior view
of a youth's rape

raw and bloody
slaughtered beef
hangs from a hook

bloody enough to cut off
all desire...

never to think of sex
not even masturbation

until it falls off
gangrened

give in
and—
and save for
death

Detail: Bacon's "Study of George Dyer"

Forget he's sitting on a stool
nude;
pay no attention to his contenance;
disregard his feet resting
on newspaper.
Nasty.
George took his life that year.
But look beyond;
be a proper critic
and seize
the day...
observe
the naked leg,
raised but bent,
in the doorway
of the room beyond
where George sits,
painted in magenta,
his face distorted
in love yet discontent.
Is that Francis himself
waiting for George
to come to bed?
The strong muscles
of these limbs...
tough, sinewy
though aging
into welfare
of the spirit.
No abstraction for him.
Death and love and bed

are real, not the surrealism,
existentialism
critics find.
The crucifix melts
in dripping blood
as the painting hangs
on the wall
as the painter rots
evolving into
a newborn dog
which will grow up
to piss on the world.

EXISTENTIAL CREED

Francis,
only two months ago
the *New York Times* reported
on your "nasty, delicious beauty."
What say there, ol' fellow,
wild artist.
Most of the world—
when I was young
and impressionable
and recognized greatness
when it suited my needs—
thought your canvas
not good enough
to wrap fish in,
let alone purchase
and hang on a livingroom wall.
Now you hang
in good places; ministers in black gowns
speak openly of your "deliciousness"
and advise the congregation
to buy tickets for the show.
Don't forget the "Screaming Pope."

And don't forget how he posed
his lover naked
on a stool centered in an empty studio
below a dangling lightbulb,
as if in a fleabag hotel—
not too different
from some folks' shitty lives.

"Sensuous paint" that if touched
would stick to the fingertip;
the scent of that paint
never to leave your nostrils,
recollection.
The touch will torment
as surely you
would have touched
the torment
Francis caught in paint,
in light and shadow
in red and black...
The scarlet of blood,
the black of hell.
Lone figures, isolated
in the center of activity
in the middle of the day,
colored in rainbows
but scented by a splash
of sour lemon.
George Dyer, brave lover,
committed suicide,
in nasty, delicious beauty...
"ultimately dazzling."

Lush language
for lush pain...tings.
I almost wrote "pain,"
which comes so easily
when considering genius.
And it does dazzle,
is delicious

but bitter,
agonizing.

Kahlo was reported
to have said,
"I'm not a Surrealist.
I never painted dreams.
I painted my own reality."
Surely this sentiment
could have been uttered
by Francis sometime
before he died in '92.

We forget Michaelangelo's sweat
and Vincent's left ear—
which he cut partially off,
and how he shot himself
in the chest. We forget
Cezanne's frustration,
the loneliness he must have suffered
for just a tad more
than comradeship.

Now that the world has acclaimed him,
we can forget how it vilified
his early labors as "horror, disconcerting."

Wait until death, my son.
my daughter,
and what now they
may think of as no more
than toilet paper

will be valued
in the thousands
 and considered
"delicious."

CARAVAGGIO PAINTING A PORTRAIT OF FRANCIS BACON

I.

in blood
sinews hang
like a medieval
boy's penis
soft
at the conjunction
of his young, angelic thigh

no
of course not...
Bacon

he was never a boy

he painted
the inner sanctum
of a boy's spirit
not with the smooth
brush
Caravaggio
held, a feather
with which
he would tickle
the young lad's
naked testicles,
though the lad was supposed
to be John, whose head
he painted on a platter,
chopped off by virtue
of the slut Salome.

II.

Bacon dropped
his trousers,
his boxer shorts
smelling of urine
and dried sperm

he covered his flesh
with magenta wax, lipstick

Caravaggio smiled, rather smirked,
turned his back on the nude painter
and continued painting
John's severed but plattered head.
and whispered,

"Francis,
pull up your pants,
you Caligula, you.
I'll meet you later.
I'm working now."

And Bacon turned
and painted
slaughtered
meat
hanging,
raw and bloody,
from a hook.

CEZANNE: "BOYS BATHING"

shocking blues
skies, mountain shoulder
and even leaves
of earthy trees
who knows the species
he finds along wanderings

The scent of blue river

blues of the eye
bright as spring,
morning, snows at dusk,
bluer than turquoise or thistle
glistening, a star in the corner
of a model's lips, the smile
of his mouth, youth shadowed
on his cheek as if brushed,
rubbings, blues never touched
by sable, the borrowed
Mediterranean

Cezanne: "Male Bather Sitting on Waterside Undergrowth"

naked lines huddle on a rock
above river sheen; one leg
bent at the knee shielding
as a fig leaf would
the man's genitals
which frighten the timid,
yet offer blues, sky blues

a line, sketched muscles
lingering above the flow
thinking perhaps of tickles
the cold might feather the toe
or thigh, or even the thought,
dream he makes, waiting
in the growth for Cezanne
to finish his own wonderings

Cezanne (In Focus)

Have fear of flesh
until the waters
wash the figure's
darker parts.

>   hands move toward water
>   through air nearly
>   touching the green of cypress,
>   grasses, shade on clouds.
>   fingers tight together,
>   almost in prayer;
>   head firm in possibility;
>   torso sleek but husky
>   as a doric pillar or tree
>   guarding bather and shore-
>   line; buttock sensually
>   suggesting male beauty

Have fear of flesh
until waters
wash and hide
the darker parts
which may
kill the joy
or cause it
to erupt

Frederick Remington

Mustache brushes spattered with beans
and coffee sticking to the bristles
which tickle the lip and the nose.
Cowboys lassoing the morning sun,
red handkerchief rubbing the throat bare
of hot sweat and crusting red dirt;
ol' boy rustling up some grub over
the open flames with his make-shift stove
leaning toward the rapid river rolling
toward the dark woods where he was sure
"injuns" were planning surprise attacks
at dawn upon the ponies tethered
to the fresh spruce air now under
falling sky of night.
                    Oh yes, we must
not forget...he also painted
Indians on bare horseback, the dirt
soon to be plastered with blood.
Indians in rich paint of many colors,
feathers down in defeat, howl like
the wolf on the mountain rock...
his last before bullets hit his throat.

"No good 'injun' unless dead," he might write,
or paint on the canvas of his faulty memory,
especially when one remembers the bristled
mustache and bucking horse
were the only images
worthy of immortality.

SARGENT'S "TOMMIES BATHING"

Privates in the British war of 1918,
he sketched, and washed their nude
bodies with watercolors on white
wove paper with the tenderness of care...
reclining in the green of tall grasses;
napping together, head to head, flesh
exposed to John's brush; teasing toes
into the blue rapids...a day away from war,
a life away from death, a breath not under
a king's command, a parent's fear.

No shame in these bodies, nude to the eyes
of God and sky; no reason to drape their flesh,
young with strength, vigor, anticipation,
or perhaps disguised of fear, bravery remaining
in the arms of their aging mothers.

On a lark. No sin except in the eye
of the beholder and surely not in Sargent's.
No sensual connotation except in the beauty
of the painter's art and the "Tommies'"
joy in the day.

Sargent: Drawing of Nicola d'Inverno

Accused of pornography...
proving dull minds blind...
yet real, sensual,
could add sensitive;
a finger might reach
and touch a slack penis,
Nicola's nipple,
his shadowed lip,
leg bent at the knee,
lush and wet.

The use of imagination:
charcoal on cream paper, or blue;
suggestion of warm lines, flesh
caressed by extraordinary art.

Where does Nicola stare?
Into what dream, fantasy,
eye which might return dreamt
glances and ease the labor
of modeling his naked body—
though we should say nude
as naked is definitely
pornographic and to be hidden—
draped from innocent eyes
which might find pleasure in

Nicola's particular
handsomeness....even the small
mustache and the curls of
his black flowing hair,

the ageless face that will
remain youthfully nineteen
until the last winds blow and sun
refuses to rise and recognize his
penis which folds between his thighs.

Or another watercolor on paper
where groin and loin are denied
to curious eyes by red drapery.
But the beauty...can we use
such a word when speaking
of a nude male...
the exquisite dedication is not
only male but Biblical which indeed
legalizes the nudity. Caravaggio
would have no problem with this
figure, nor would Bacon shiver
and avert his eyes.

SARGENT: "STUDY OF A MALE NUDE"

No Michelangelo burst of might and strength
nor a handsome movie star; no brute
of a Spanish bull or toreador...
simply a male figure reclining with his right
leg bent at the knee, his groin draped
with an extended arm raised
behind the youth's head, left arm clothed
by the red drape. Eyes closed, mouth tight,
slender figure exposed, vulnerable. As though
finished with making love, complete; asleep
from concerns, confident in his pleasure
and will never awaken to further joys,
glad to expose his maleness to the eye
which might find him resting
at the bottom of the stairs...
or is Sargent interested only in shapes,
lines of the figure enhanced by red drapes.

PISSARO: TROPICAL IMPRESSIONS

The young lad
carrying
the huge jug
atop his head
with a thin smile,
a pencil line,
simple, direct
from the artist's brush.

What does he carry
in his jug,
and so far,
lemon juice, quince
or some strange beverage
only he and his mother know?

(Witch. Bruja. Sorcerer.)

What does he carry
in the pail
in his right hand?
Milk from a cow or goat,
tamarind juice,
avocado seeds
for planting,
rumtumrum.
That's what it is...
rum.
Hence the smile
penciled by the artist.
Oh, I know that smile

very well. I have
seen it on my mouth,
my own purple lips
tasting of rum
under moonlight.

I'll tell only
the man with the paint and brush
as he sits by my Caribbean
with my warm waters on his
paint-spattered cheek.
What is in my pail?
Perhaps mangoes
under the moon.

His sketch.
I see his green cheek
shaded by the pencil;
I see his dark eyes
shadowed;
I feel his darkness,
mystery,
brownness,
as though I could reach
and pinch the flesh of his arm
or cheek.

But then I might spill
the contents of my jug,
of my pail,
and then
my mother would whip me.

Camille,
there are virgins yet,
though they carry no jugs
nor buckets nor pails
of rumtumrum;
they remain
rainbows,
though as you remember
there were/are few
rainbows
as there was/is
so little rain,
but when it rained
he would throw down the jug,
she would throw down the jug,
drop the pail on naked earth
and dance between the rain drops.

Each pore of my black skin
absorbs the little fingers
and I glisten,
spotted in the silver
of cool rain,
and I tingle, tickled
by those tropical hands.

As we all danced within the rain
to Danish tunes,
salt-free end cool,
and we knew
we would drink again
the sweet gift of the clouds,

of the gods,
and so he danced
and she danced
and we danced
the village danced
the whole island danced
in absolute delight
danced naked feet
beautiful flesh
spattered with rainbows.

And you Camille Pissarro
stood there and watched
as the young girls
and the young boys
swayed
in voluptuous rhythms
and old women
with sagging breasts
and fishermen
with stringers of fish
and jugs of rum
or lime juice
resting sagely on the earth
(now running blood).

"Impressions.
Only impressions.
I have a lifetime
of memories.
See my pictures.
My painted poems,

my sensual drawing
of the sensuous boy
(you should have seen him
prancing down the street
with the jug on his head
and his feet stomping,
kicking up the island dust,
the tropical dust)
yes, my painted poems,
smiles in pencil.
How dare they write
so arrogantly
on my impressions."

We digested it all...
the rum to this moment
spills from my lips,
runs sticky and sweet
down my chin,
anticipating rain
and the exotic dance
the sensuous sway
of our bodies
to the beat of the rain
drumming the dusty earth.

I would dance in papaya juice.
I would dance in lime juice
I would dance in a thunder clap
I would dance and make lightning

I will always carry the jug and pail
and my smile will taunt the ages.
Witch me if you will.
Witch me if you must
Pencil my lips
I will dance and dance under rain.

Remember the sweaty days
and the sweltering nights
under a hot tropical moon
that stole sleep.
Remember iguanas,
lizards, white chameleons
on whitewashed walls
of the cottage high
on the palm-treed hillside
overlooking the blue bay,
overlooking the vast
peacock-blue harbor,
mysterious spinnakers
striking gongs as the Caribbean
breezed across the patio
gently shaking the mango
to a soft tremble,
to music, rhythm of the isle.

I walked into his sketch
forever a boy
as I have strolled into this poem
forever a boy,
as though the witch,
the bruja,

the jumm jumm
had tranced me into this future,
onto this page of history

"And I would observe him move
down the dusty path, the road,
his jug jiggling
on his unsteady head because
of his odd dancing gait
on unsturdy legs,
listing beneath the heavy pail,
kicking up dust,
the bloody dust settling
on hibiscus blooms, cactus,
bougainvillea,
the sweet pencil smile
which drew my attention
I mean to be ever there,
the charcoal cheek
with or without rainbows
as you say... but I
can't recall rainbows
in those Virgin Islands
and his heavy-breasted mother
somewhere ahead down the dirt road
cooking green bananas,
bacalao and yams
with a sprinkle of salt.
a swash of olive oil,
a toss of raw onion rings.
The choice meal sits on her table,
which will certainly bring an additional smile."

I hope you tasted that good tropical food
as you recorded the 19th Century
with pencil and charcoal and oil,
recorded the smile,
the jug and pail,
and that sweet black face,
and what was behind that African smile.
I hope you had the inclination
to wonder if one day
a hundred or more
years later we would be sitting
at my typewriter talking
of this child. It would/will
rekindle memories in my imagination
of the frangipani, iguanas,
the pomegranates,
the melons sweet and orange
hanging from my tree
when my neighbors' monkey
would allow the papaya to hang,
oh yes, and the rum nights
and coconut days by the sea,
the rain and the occasional rainbow
and the dances....
the days of dancing with naked feet
on the wet earth or slippery walks....
dancing naked, the carnival

I walked into his sketch
etched forever
on the front page
of the New York Times.

No storm from the sea,
nor sandstorm from the shore,
nor rain and lightning from the sky
can ever, will ever erase
the smile he penciled
onto his canvas,
you typed onto the paper.
My mother heaves her breasts
and laughs, the wood floor
of our shack jiggling
like the jug he sketched
onto my head

Yes. I can hear her.

"I hear her laugh, too."

She laughs so hard
and stomps the wood
floor so hard the rats
run out into the sunshine,
the coconuts shake,
an avocado falls,
the chickens cluck,
the goat baas,
and the mule brays

Better that my mouth
will always
carry the smile,
that my jug and pail
will always be full

and my mother in her misery
will always laugh
and jar an avocado down
and make a chicken cluck.

"Amen."

Amen.

My father will always
be fishing,
and the bacalao will always
be drying on the line
blowing in the Caribbean breeze.
and I will always walk
the waterfront
dreaming of far-off countries
and other islands
where other boys
carry jugs of exotic juices
atop their heads.
And their mothers will always
be placing good food
on what could be
an empty table.

PART II
LINES ON PAPER

It is a wise man who knows his father.
—Sir Francis Bacon

IN MEMORY OF MY FATHER,
ANDREW ANTHONY KENNY

SKETCH

I'm trying to sketch his portrait,
trying to draw a picture
of a man I don't understand,
perhaps never knew,
a man who refuses to leave
my nights, the darkness
of my life. He wanders, softly
speaks, suggests different routes,
channels, ways of moving
into a July dawn, an August eve
when bats swirl, seeking
mosquitoes beneath the portico.

I sketch a wide forehead under
a hank of chestnut-colored hair,
sea-blue eyes, a substantial nose
that cannot deny its beginnings
miles away on a reservation in Canada
that only his mother knew.

I'm sketching a man
I, perhaps, never knew
just an outline of a man
who, fully-fleshed,
would be colored
in humaness,
in fatherness,
not just this scent
of flowers rotting
on his grave.

I'm trying to sketch a man
with mo(u)rnings and afternoons,
a man who loved to fish and hunt,
drink beer, make love night after night
with any woman who would disrobe,
curl beside his thigh, his chest.

Already this portrait is a sham.
Fling it into the fire,
burn its lies.
Only in memory, which fades,
does this portrait hang, nailess,
on the walls of death...black
and so soundless that not a single
footstep is heard on the air.
But he is there, you know he is,
listening, watching every step.

Ragina

What was she doing out of context...
the story, history, the fact,
the fact that Native women did not marry
those pink-faced, pinched noses
for any reason...surely not love,
especially as he was just off the boat
and she was not a captive like her
great-great-grandmother Eunice West,
taken by force in 1711 and held in the stout
arms of some handsome Mohawk...
the very thing of which romance is made.

Her ticket to New America
came with an Irish brogue.
And here we are...a brood, at last,
for his name shall die and her name
shall cease to be and only the mewl
of a scraggly cat will be heard in the night,
mixing with his death rattle, which
rose and gurgled for nine dark nights
and nine dark days until someone placed
a pillow gently on his face and handed
his gold watch to the empty sweaty palm.
Ah, history, you're the scoundrel where
the blame has come to rest, where the sins
of omission and the sins of action
dwell in the heart and hide in the spirit.

She crossed into New America blameless
and innocent, and March came down with
fury and the blizzard covered the footprints

as he strode from his raw cabin to her lodge
with not a single flower tight in his hand.
Did she have a choice?
Bad times there were: no work, no work,
no work for Indian man, woman, or child.
And so she said, with bent head, "Yes, I will,"
and suddenly there stood Cecile, Julia,
and the boy child, Andrew Anthony, as red
of skin as his mother was brown.
She never forgot to sing them lullabies,
told them stories of Brother Wolf
and Cowardly Thrush. She breathed
a million years into his young lungs,
breathed health, and as much wisdom as
she might summon in her song. Story
after story fell from her lips, the way
Skywoman fell from the Spirit World
and through the vast net of stars
to Turtle's back, clutching
a strawberry vine in her fist.
And this is how his world commenced.

March Gift

Like most little boys, he came head first,
screaming, kicking the sides of her womb,
thrashing and begging for independence,
hairless, toothess, the day-old monster
already knew where he was going and where
he had just come from. Probably not much
different from any other newborn,
except that there seemed an extra sense
of defiance, will, a strength of scream
few lads bring into this world at birth.
He would never need to struggle, fight
for strength...it was God-given, or thrust
upon him by the will of the Creator, as though
he were Skywoman's first-born twins,
one good, the other evil. He would carry
the tooth of wolverine and the scent
of the wood lily until death.
An auspicious beginning: a ferocious
March storm dragged him screaming
into his mother's arms to nestle in warmth
under sisters' eyes and a gruff father-voice
till the day she could no longer be his protection.

Then the sky fell, and all hell broke loose...

GRANDMA

I do not know the stories
her hands told a January night
before the pot-bellied stove,
the hound wiggling its sleepy
nose as close to the fire
as its hind-end dared,
not the song she sang when winter
winds blew against the kitchen
windows, or dandelions danced
across the front yard under
lilac and dogwood. Nor am I sure
of the herbs she sought, picked,
to cure a common cold, bitter
aches somewhere in childhood;
my tongue never tasted the wild
blackberries her hands, stained
with blood from the thorns,
picked, eager to please with jam,
or pie or crisp, picked under
the coveting eye of bear
sitting in the darkness of waiting,
prepared to crash through brush
to save his August breakfast.
Not once did her palm pass
my fevered brow, prayers lift
for this child's recovery,
never did she hold me tight
in her embrace while dancing
in the Longhouse snowy evenings
while the water drum banged
and rattles rattled, assuring the people

the village was safe and well supplied
with the venison and maple sugar men
hunted and gathered for the Nation.

This good woman did not stay long
enough to hear my *adowe*, my gift
found along the way, which would
bring a smile to her aging face.
I hope my father found the prayer
feathers, colors of day, song
of the twilight thrush which pleased
and caused a twinkle in her eye,
and that she knows our stories.

GRANDPA

I.
I suppose he
          was there,
but possibly he
          was with
the boys, knowing
          the cries
would tear his
          heart
and no drink
          could ever
block the nose
          of a new birth.

But behold—
          a son!
Drink up, men!
          What else
can an Irish father do,
          especially one
who'd been caught
          between
the rough sea
          and the fear
of the new land
          looming ahead,
where a native woman
          waited
with warm covers
          on a bed
of corn husks and straw.

Grandpa landed
    within sight
of the elm, the great elm
    listing
toward the white pine
    where they met,
and shortly after
    the cries
were heard and the jug
    of stout
was lifted
    at the birth.

II.
I am to tell
    the story.

What have I forgotten...
what will I forget.
But what will I remember...?

EUCHRE

Nine o'clock was pretty late
to Grandpa. Cows needed milking
early at five a.m., haying would wait
for the lad to down the gruel,
a cup of black coffee and a deep
cut of breath. Grandpa did
not have any tolerance
for young lads going out on the town,
even if it were only a card game
at the church. He walked to town,
not far by miles, untied his horse
and the buggy the lad had driven
to the montly euchre party, and drove it home.
He'd teach that boy a lesson...
nine o'clock, indeed. At ten the boy
was amazed to find the horse and buggy
gone, but he knew his father pretty well
and commenced the three miles home.
Seeing the oil lamp in the kitchen,
he knew better than to go in,
and went to the hay barn to sleep.

When he awoke, the barn flamed
from the cigarette he'd hand-rolled
before he drifted into sleep.
His arm badly burned, he rose
and left the farm, a father who surely
would have beaten him within an inch
of his life. Without coin, luggage, or a kiss
from his stepmother, Agnes, he flew
down the road to the ferry boat
on the St. Lawrence to seek shelter

with Aunt Libbie, whom he knew
would take him in.

In no time, he was laboring as a waterboy,
and didn't return to Grandpa
until he had won a wife, made three
kids, and paid for his own new Chevrolet.
Success, he knew, would save him
from a beating he surely deserved.

1914

Hands and pockets empty,
skies wide and blue,
youth rich in dreams,
world open for exploration
and discovery.

What does a teenager do
in a year like that...

Picnics and rowboat excursions,
cake auctions, trout fishing
in Adirondack streams.

Lots of mischief, trouble.
Arms to break in cherry trees,
and girls to find, girls who
will not care that there
are no chin whiskers yet.

Streets are safe from
drugs, gangs, hate,
and bazaars and festivals
take the place of horror films
and porn shops.

And yet there was
no innocence...

Back alleys spotted with blood,
coat hangers left behind.
War brooded in the heavens.

Clouds were darkening, thunder
and lightning were building,
but the Christian God was there,
and He watched while the pagans
shivered in fear and dread.

World War I

He claimed to have been
in the Army, but I never found
a uniform packed up in a musty
old metal trunk, nor did Uncle Warren
ever speak of his duty overseas.
He loved to tell the tale of how
at seventeen he'd signed up to go
"over there" to fight for freedom,
but the ship, as it sailed across
the Atlantic, was wired the news
that Armistice had been declared.
The ship, he claimed, caught in a storm
in the northern waters, turned around
and headed back to port in New York City.
He'd laugh, showing his missing tooth,
his glasses sliding down his nose,
and we'd never mention that we knew
Indians weren't naturalized until 1924.

THE DEPRESSION

Franklin Delano Roosevelt,
the C.C.C. and Social Security.
Help was on the way.

He didn't bring the men
and their families
down from Kanawake
but when two men,
two women and a horde of kids
arrived, he got them jobs.
Ditch digging was all he could
offer, but they didn't complain.

Hunger is an ugly thing.
He knew it from his days
as a waterboy. Too young to work
iron to build the American dream.
he later encouraged the Indian men
to climb high in good spirit/balance
to the great skies where
the Haudenosaunee lived in harmony.

And in his own way,
he touched that sky
Help was where they found him.

Enterprenaur

Waterboy to ditchdigger
at sixteen, and seventy-five cents
a day, with only book two schooling,
by his wedding day in '21
he was driving a city truck
and he rented a city-owned
house for Doris and kids
who would surely arrive.
It didn't take long for him
to hit on an idea of how
to make money. He'd drag
the creeks for minnows
and sell them to the men
from Utica. Nickels and dimes
poured in, enough to buy
a second-hand truck.
He hired a brother-in-law to cut
green wood and stack it behind
the house, where he'd sell it,
cord by cord, to his neighbors.

One Saturday morning he drove
his truck down to the dealer's
and drove home in a shiny
midnight ebony Chevrolet.
Not too long after, he stood
in front of his own business,
a roadside restaurant with a huge
sign: ANDY'S PLACE. He soon had
a small empire of Sunoco stations,
a brand new house, a different wife,
and a fat bank account. But he'd worked

his way up to bad eyesight
and several strokes, and though
he passed to his Creator in style,
pain filled every part of his soul.

Photo

It sits on the second shelf
from the top, not too dusty,
surrounded by my books.
He's dressed in a proper suit
and tie, and, I must add, very
handsome. Standing slightly behind
my surly-looking mother, he wears
a sneaky little shit-eating grin.
My poor mother wears what looks
like a bowl with a feather on her head.
She has a fox draped around
her shoulders. She later confided that it
belonged to the photographer, who loaned
it to make her appear a bit more sophisticated,
and that even the hat was borrowed.
She was sullen, she said, because his hand
was smack against her bottom, and she knew
she'd pay dearly for her dinner.

There's a bouquet of flowers,
possibly daisies, but the photograph
is dark, predicting bad times ahead
for one or both. Wearisome clouds
are on the horizon behind them,
and the bow around her neck looks
a little too tight. She's not happy
in this setting. Too late.

In moments they'll be off
on their happy honeymoon.

HONEYMOON

He rented a motorcycle. She hated
the thought, petrified. His cousin
and best friend, Lonnie, also rented
a cycle and came along, his girlfriend
gripping his waist from the back of the seat.

The girls, though terrified, did manage
to laugh. Why was the best friend going
on the honeymoon with the newlyweds?
To the day she passed, Doris couldn't figure
that out. But she was in love and allowed
it to happen. She chalked it up
to being Andy's way of showing
his strength and control.

Near Rochester, Lonnie swerved,
the cycle crashed, and he and Maryann
were slaughtered. Andy turned.
The couple never made Niagara Falls,
nor found real happiness in marriage,
though love and sex were heated.

Pregnant

He had her pregnant most of the time.
High libido...he did not know the term.
He knew only the urge was there driving
him nuts. Her thoughts on the subject
didn't matter much. He brought home
the bacon, and why did two people
live together if not so the female
could cater to the male's every demand.
She had a tough time, time and time again.
Only God knew how many brothers
I was supposed to have had.
Miscarriage. Stillborn. Aborted...
She hated the water he loved,
despised the summer cottage,
loathed and mistrusted the idea
of his being in town alone all week...
and it's hard to believe she didn't
wonder with whom while she
was cooped up with the kids
miles from town,
and pregnant to boot.
Not fun.

Name

They named me Maurice,
pronounced Morris,
as though I were
British,
and I wore it—
a bloodied bandage—
as a warrior's shield,
and there were many battles
behind the church,
in the one-room school,
later in the pub
or wherever
boys and men gathered
to roust and joke
and tear skin off
knuckles to prove
nothing.

My name was Maurice,
pronounced Morris,
until I went to war
and changed it back.

O those sweet breasts
nourishing
to his wet lips,
breasts
would remain
warm and nourishing
(the bar maid
the friend's best girl
the beauty on the beach
the little woman's friend
and yes, of yes, the wife)
his swagger told the unmitigated
truth: a quiet womanizer

Mama

She woke me
a moment before dawn. We sat
at the bottom of their bed,
I no more than six, facing
the window which had a long, wide
view over the poplars in the backyard
and beyond the railroad tracks snaking
off toward Canada. She remained quiet
for a while, though she managed to direct
my attention to a car parked behind the fence.
Her index finger pointed north
and she murmured in my ear, "That's
your father there with a woman.
He's kissing her, making love."
I heard that repeated night after night,
the same horrid words, whispered
in my ear, locking me forever more,
forever more, into the prison of self.

CHANGE

We loved those Friday nights
when he'd come lurching home
after too many beers, stumble
into tables, spilling black coffee,
dancing on one foot at a time
as Mama tried to pull off his pants
at the bottom of the stairs.
Dimes and nickels would tinkle
out, and my sisters and I became
rich. It meant a Saturday matinee,
chocolate bars, licorice sticks.
But most of all, it convinced us
that he was in a happy mood
and would sleep so long he'd never
know the nuns sent home a note
to say that I'd been bad in class,
had wet my pants, never mentioning
that I'd raised my hand and asked
and had been refused.

That Time

he left me in the Chevy
while he went hunting rabbits,
tracks across the damp meadow

    (the hound smell
    glows on the leather seat
    and its breath stains the glass

    dry corn stalks dance
    in a nearby field
    cedar scents
    the woody afternoon,
    oak and ash
    finger November and my spine

    I hear his shot.
    Mama didn't want me
    to be around guns
    or to make friends of hounds)

I was afraid of dead rabbits
and their bloody smell,
but he came from the woods
blood on his hands
and blood on his face

and I knew we'd live a little
longer...its blood was still
warm...despite Mama.

My Sixth August

My father wades the moning river
tangled in colors of the dawn.
He drags a net through the cold
water, spits tobacco juice,
and stumbles. Light warns the minnows
that hide under bullheads. Sharp air
smells of wild lobelia and apple.

In my sixth August, a kingfisher
rattles from a willow. I am too
busy picking iris in the wet field
to know a game warden shakes his head
above us on the narrow bridge to home.
The west wind has trapped our scent,
and light prisons our mobile hands.

Hunting, 1933

Pheasants
ovened behind corn bread

Guns stacked
against the wall
tilt toward the china
closet, a glint of light
blasts from the woodstove,
cracking fire as she lifts
the iron lid.

A child braids golden
feathers into dusters,
has slipped a cobalt
into her brother's hatband
bound by squirrel pelt
beside crow feather,
partridge feather,
a chipmunk tail.

Boys stand around in socks
chew pork skins, dried currants,
probably considering the buck
they'll bag next month.

Summer sweetgrass scents
the meaty kitchen
reminding the older women
of arthritic knees and cut fingers.

The man of the house snores,
rocking chair
thumping the floor—
faint thunder possibly predicting snow.

Two supper birds,
October gold,
russet of the field where grain,
forgotten wheat, caught an eye
and silenced breath.

A Winter Kitchen Scene

Smell of rabbit's blood is on the air;
its chill bites the young chin. He grins
and pokes mother with his game. She jumps
back frightened but knowing
she'll have to clean the animal for roasting
with a few potatoes, some carrots,
an onion, perhaps. His hounds' tails wag
hard against her legs in a happiness
as pronounced as his joy. They, too,
are proud and they, too, await a good supper
for the cries, tearing of the woods,
searching the scent, the kill.

She does her man right. Tears off the fur
which she can turn into mittens, singes
the skin on the stove's flame, pulls out
the guts for the dogs with her own grunt
and groan. This is not her favorite way
to spend an afternoon when the soaps
are on the radio and Ma Perkins has lost
her wedding ring. But she does
as she has been told. Shortly, supper
will be on the table with, as always,
a plate of cheese, a jar of homemade
pickles, butter sweating in salt,
and her bread.

Winter night shifts down upon the house
as children come to the table, grouchy
they must cease their play to eat an animal
they'd rather see hopping in the woods.

He commands the moment for silence.
Eat what the Creator has given you
and be thankful.
      Supper over, sleep now,
fire stoked, lights out, dogs
outside huddling in the cold.
He turns under the heavy quilts,
sighs and throws his weight
to heavy dreams, tomorrows.

Water Drum

To my knowledge
he never beat
the drum
nor sang
in the Longhouse
but he told stories
over bowls of popcorn
and sang in my mother's
kitchen..."If I had the wings
of a turtle, over these prison
walls I would fly."
I knew the line was wrong,
but I wasn't going to be
the one to tell him.
I wish he'd beaten
that water drum
and offered his song
in the Longhouse night.

BAYONNE, NEW JERSEY

A boy new in town
          at ten
in a field smelling
          of oil
hears the crash
          of drums
then comes upon a leg
          long and naked
jutting through
          tall grass,
then fat thigh,
          soft genitals,
fright speaks
          of death,
knowledge of alcohol.
          Ten now.
Must call
          someone,
          someone.

POLITICS

He didn't like his cinder driveway,
so he called the right department
and shortly it was paved
by a bottle of scotch.
He didn't like where the street
lamp stood, the light not shining
on his parking lot. Another
phone call, two more bottles
of scotch and the light
fell where he wanted it to.

He claimed he wasn't a politician
but he'd worked many a year
for the city and knew all
the department bosses pretty well.

As a lad fresh from Canada
pimpled probably, certainly
strangely pronouncing *out* and *house*,
he came to live with Aunt Libbie
at first, then Mrs. Collins
on elegant State Street,
her house a gas station now.

He came with burns on his arms,
just one clean shirt and large stars
in his eyes. The new frontier, eternity
perhaps immortality. But he was met
with the job of waterboy, fifty cents a day,
which barely paid for Mrs. Collins' rent
and a few packs of cigarettes,
let alone a bottle of beer or a date

with a pretty teenage American girl
fresh off the farm. But he knew how to smile
and wink and beguile.
Ever the politician, he knew
all lights could be moved.

PRICES

Butter fifteen cents a pound.
He screamed bloody murder
when she brought home two pounds,
sweaty and salty to his taste.
He yelled and stomped the kitchen
floorboards when he walked
in from work and found her
at the stove frying hamburgers
and hash browns with no apron
covering a spanking new orange dress
impressed with forget-me-nots.
Her simple, honest response: *I wanted
to look pretty when you came home.*
He fromped to the table, picked up
his fork and skewered the hunk
of yellow cheese he always insisted
on having on the table with a dish
of pickles, a supper ritual, a must,
no matter what the cost.

FATHER'S DAY

He didn't believe in it,
nor Mother's Day,
nor Easter.
Just a day to waste
money on silly ties,
or flowers,
or feathered hats,
pink rabbits
or purple chicks
which have nothing
to do with Christ.
He didn't belive in it,
and he wasn't cheap.

Mean

I don't know what I might have done
wrong or bad. Maybe it was when
I broke the door window after my sister
Mary tried to take a butcher knife
to me for calling her a dirty name,
or maybe when I kicked my older sister
Agnes in the stomach when she took
all the chocolate fudge my dad had made
for all of us to her locked bedroom.

Whatever. He took me out back,
said, "Break off a switch from the black willow,"
then pulled back my ear and beat. I screamed,
"I hope I die!" He beat harder. I thought
my ear would just drop to the ground.

He forgot that day that Native men
do not whip their children. They lead
by example. But he didn't kill my spirit.
I'm still rotten mean.

STRANGE LOVE

His protection beat scars
on her legs and arms.
Mama left the house,
Grandma cried in her room.
I hid in a dark closet.
                    Years later,
she forgave him with a pair
of pajamas for Christmas
and an expensive birthday card.
The same young man over whom
he beat her, married her and paid
not for just groceries but all the bills,
even paid for the pajamas and the card.

COMPLICATED

His knife drew blood
that his hand wiped off.

TRAVEL

He'd always wanted to scent
the cherry blossoms in D.C.;
he'd always yearned to see Alaska,
to fish for salmon, see a polar bear.
He always wanted to spend his days
and nights at his Chaumont Bay
cottage where he could boat home
to Canada across the lake if he wished.
            He got to St. Louis once.
And he took the ferry home
to his father's funeral.

INDIANA

How many times would he start
the Chevy, pile in his disappointments,
chew a little crow thinking
things would get better. Pills worked,
and doctors had cures, but he
actually knew the best medicine.
He shook my hand and paid a friend
to drive me out to Indiana
where hopes and dreams
had half a chance.

And Back

That time he didn't come.
He sent them out instead
He sent Pat and Mary to Indiana
where they packed up my pills,
some patches of doggerel,
a hamper of dirty clothes,
and in silence drove us
home to the north country.
That wasn't the first time
he came for me. He came
to Alex Bay the summer
grease paint caught my whim.
He found me sleeping
in an old garage and washing
dishes in a hot Italian kitchen,
steaming with the scents
of pasta, tomatoes and chicken.
He brought me home then,
somewhat mystified at how
I could carry so much weight
when I could barely carry anything
at home. But insanity reigned
in this teenager's mind, and off
he let me go again, to Broadway
dreams that melted into nightmares.
Once more he came to take me home,
broken, to the mucilage that waited there.
College seemed the right thing to do
for the next few years, but he didn't come
this time. He sent them out instead
to rescue me in muggy Indiana.

The Hill

How strange, this same lonely hill
topped with aging cedars and broken
headstones in the graveyard obviously
reeking with ghosts and family history:
which woman should he marry now
that old age was settling in?
How could I know which one
would make him happy? Both were old
or slowly getting there. One made money
during World War II in ammunitions.
The other was just plain rich;
I didn't know how, nor did I care.
I thought he should return to my mother.
I knew he loved her, still.

We spoke on the very same hill I'd ride
to on my horse, to sit, let the good dreams
roll out, imagine the world awaited
and that it would soon be mine.
Faith can be a terrible thing,
especially the blind. That very same hill
where on the dirt road behind the cedars
I first made love in his car one summer night,
never realizing that not even that would ever
come true, now reeked of dust and piss.
He showed me, when he asked my permission
to marry, that there was no love, and sex
was a disappointment which created only
burning nights and a wintry world of loss.

It Didn't Make Any Difference

He was gonna teach us...
my sisters and me...how to swim
in the lake...as my mother screamed
and flailed her arms in summer air.
She hated with a passion
the cottage at Chaumont Bay...a camp
he near worshipped and we kids adored
from late June to late August. He knew
he was right, my mother wrong;
it was done only for our good and safety.
He'd load us into the rowboat
one at a time, me last as the youngest
of three, row out twenty or fifty feet,
dump the kid overboard, and force
a swim home. If you didn't know how
you'd learn on the spot was his philosophy.
Later he gave us cigars to smoke
and vomit. Then he brought
out the whiskey bottle and forced
us to drink until drunk,
and very sick. I became
an alcoholic at age six.
It didn't work so well, but he...
he had good intentions.

As A Father

He was good to his kids:
new clothes for September school,
dolls and sleds and books
about Tarzan in his African jungle,
though he believed the best toys
were sticks and stones and friends.
He bought a tricycle, smashed to bits
when a nephew left it on the railroad tracks,
then an Elgin two-wheeler that carried us
to public school. He saw two girls
through Catholic high school,
one boy through undergraduate years,
and left him enough when he died
for a year in the wild Caribbean Islands.
What more could a father do?

In the Box

I don't remember how he looked in death.
Was his ruddy cheek waxed, his eye open
with a wink? Did he wear a toothless grin,
or was he sober, somber, at rest?
Now I wonder if they'll wax my smile,
poke me down into white or blue satin.
They'd better screw the lid down tight.
I won't go gently.

Were there flowers...it was March?
Were there mass cards? He'd been
excommunicated by a priest with wine
stains on his vestments. Were there pretty
ladies crying at the bier...those he'd loved
were probably gone. I want iris at my box,
and lilac. It's doubtful there'll be a priest
or mass cards, not for me. Ladies? A few.

I don't need to remember how he looked in death.
In memory I see him hunting in the woods,
with a pole at his favorite lake or stream,
or on Friday nights when he tilted from a beer
or two, and we kids gathered the coins he
spilled on the way to bed. More lines
for the sketch, the portrait of a father
that can never be complete

To Death

She
      loved
           him;
           the facts
     of
life.

       . . .

He

carried
her pretty face

in the pocket of death,
clutching the sound
of her name.

Many Years Later

Night after night I wrestle
with his voice. He continues
to believe I'm the weak son.
I remember so well being home
from the university and watching
together a murder mystery on TV.
Before it was over, he left the living
room and shuffled off to the kitchen.
He'd been ill for three or four years,
heart attack, strokes, you name it.
I could hear odd sounds coming
from the kitchen, sounds as though
someone in there was crying...
But I survived, I'm strong.
Why couldn't he believe in me?
To this very moment I hear those sobs.
Sometimes I think they are my own.

SOMETIMES, INJUSTICE

The day I was born my father bought me a .22.
A year later my mother traded it for a violin.
Ten years later my big sister traded that
for a guitar and gave it to her boyfriend...
who sold it.

Now you know why I never learned to hunt,
or learned how to play a musical instrument,
or became a Wall Street broker.

The Same

If it had been possible
to choose a different father,
who would you have chosen?
Frank Sinatra, Chief Sitting Bull,
President Lincoln, Gary Cooper,
or maybe Babe Ruth! Would you
want to choose someone different,
or learn to understand the man
you've grown and groaned with all
your life, the man who picked you up
when a baby with wet diapers, the man
who taught you how to swim and ride
a bike, and drive a car. The man who sawed
down the Christmas tree and hung the lights,
who brought the piglet home and raised it
to slaughter in the coal cellar, the man
who fought battles with Gramma Herrick for you,
bought the first bookcase, and the old horse
who lived for two days after he brought her home.
Why do you want to change him? What makes you think
anyone else would be better? You surely would
not be the same. You might stand six feet tall instead
of five feet five. You might have become a fireman,
a gangster, a movie star. Who would have been your
mother, and would you have loved her more?
What makes you think your life would have been
better. Would you change it if you could?

Mask

He stands at the edge of pine,
grinning though missing a tooth.
The hunter's cap, his red-checked jacket
smelling of hundreds of hunts.
He stands at the edge...
he will stand there as long
as I have dreams when I sleep.

I smell his coat, scent of deer, pheasant,
grouse. A spatter of blood rides his right
cheek, his left hand holds a rifle, the right
tugs on a line of bloody game, rabbits
Mama will stew for supper, sew the fur
into winter mittens or muffs.

He stands at the edge of pine
as darkness and quiet drop behind him.
He offers no words, yet smiles,
eyes atwinkle. I need to hear his words,
warm in the evening air. I need
his gift of words, images for me to slip
deeper into comforting dreams.

He moves into the woods, the darkness
of the pines. He lifts his gun, drags his line
of bloody rabbits. I shout for him to wait.
He stops, turns, beckons me to follow. I wake,
knowing he'll return and not just beckon but speak,
urging me to follow him into darkness.

ESSENCE

I am the blood of this grass
which feeds maggots
that will consume my flesh.
I will return to this field
and my blood will feed the red
berries ripening under spring.

Grass are my eyes
and I look into the years
of desolation out of ruin.
Blood will spill on rock,
dry winds will sweep
its red dust into space.

My eyes are crows
who laugh in the early
of morning slanting across
elm boughs which have no right
to grow in mountain soil.

Crows are my black wings.
Crows are white winter.
Their caw is darkness.
The darkness is the ebony rose
that wilts in the summer hand.

The hand is the receptacle of blood.
From the fingers, cries
of creation stream...hawk,
berry, pine, trout
of old mountain creek.

My mountain is the mystery
of all seasons...now thick
in snow, cold to noon,
pink of falling light
striking the bare tamarack
and rusting cedar.

Cedar is where my mother
sleeps, her bones brittle
and cracked by rod and spade.
She will never pick berries again,
nor kiss my father's lips.

Berries are blood
thinning in veins.
I will eat grass, gain
strength to combat
maggots buried deep
in muscles of my thighs.

My father will step out
from snow, create
summer of December.
He will replace the grass.

GOING HOME

The book lay unread in my lap
snow gathered at the window
from Brooklyn it was a long ride
the Greyhound followed the plow
from Syracuse to Watertown
to country cheese and maples
tired rivers and closed paper mills
home to gossipy aunts...
their dandelions and pregnant cats...
home to cedars and fields and boulders
cold graves under willow and pine
home from Brooklyn to the reservation
that was not home
to songs I could not sing
to dances I could not dance
from Brooklyn bars and ghetto rats
to steaming horses and stamping frozen earth
barns and privies lost in blizzards
home to a Nation, Mohawk
to faces I did not know
and hands that did not recognize me
to names and doors
my father shut

NORTH

In memory of my father

sun rises over mountain lakes
fox breakfasts in the berry patch
mice tug grains into the burrow
grass has a way of growing

north by the old trail
north by the Susquehanna
north by the Freeway
north by the Alleghany or Mohawk
airlines that sweep out into north country,
deerland, Thousand Islands;
north by semis that scoop up the north
and wrap its aluminum foil about
your Thanksgiving turkey
and cool your pudding in the refrigerator

north by any path would be north
north...by north star, northern
northern country of villages and cowpens
cheese factories and crab apples, trout,
diseased elms and sick roots
fenced meadows slit by snowmobiles
sky cracked by television wires,
and hunters blizzard to cabins
by dead deer...the last kept
them abandoned in the north snow
from home in Staten Island

north of strawberry fields, milkweed
north of maples running sap to boil
north, north country, northern New York

where corn grew to the table and squash
and bean covered the valleys
north of strawberry fields, north of sumac
north of smoke, north of tomorrow, today
of yesterday that was and is and will be
for strawberries grow forever
and wolves will cross the frozen river
under the flight of geese

sun humps over hills and horses
muskrat in the stream
swimming to shore
with a mouthful of mud
the bee sipping honey
minnows in the creek

grass has a way of growing
north, north along the old trail

guard the eastern gate.

My Father Does Not Sing

The oncoming dark catches breath;
even in the dream the Medicine Man
passes the dark along to another.
No Pow Wow, but a carnival stretched
into a raw theater with men chased
out and off the midway.

But Dark. My, oh so frightening Dark.
I cannot find the Medicine Woman
for her herbs and rocks and charms
though we know she is waiting.

Shirley, not recognized at first,
says to wait for the Holy Woman
as she will appear and replace
my father, who neither speaks nor sings
in the dream, in the dark. I wake
in folds of sheets, the radio blowing
a flute, tip over a plastic bottle
of ginger ale and dawn slides
through the darkness.
I wake and wait.

Notes on the Poems

Sir Francis Bacon (1561–1626) - English philosopher, statesman, and essayist, his most famous aphorism is "Knowledge is power." His works established and popularized an inductive methodology for scientific inquiry. Various scholars have stated that he was the illegitimate son of Queen Elizabeth and Robert Dudley, Earl of Leicester, and that he was homosexual. He is the author of the epigraphs that begin each section of this book.

Francis Bacon - Francis Bacon (1909 – 1992) was an Anglo-Irish figurative painter. He was a collateral descendant of Sir Francis Bacon. His artwork is well known for its bold, austere, and often grotesque or nightmarish imagery.

George Dyer - In the 1960s, British painter Francis Bacon surprised a burglar in his home and invited him to share his bed. The burglar, a working-class man named George Dyer, was thirty years Bacon's junior. He remained Bacon's lover until his suicide in 1971 on the evening before Francis Bacon's major retrospective in the Grand Palais in Paris,

Cezanne - Paul Cezanne (1839–1906) was a French artist and Post-Impressionist painter whose work laid the foundations for the transition from 19th century art to the radically different art of the 20th century.

Michelangelo - Michelangelo di Lodovico Buonarroti Simoni (1475 – 1564), commonly known as Michelangelo, was an Italian Renaissance painter, sculptor, architect, poet and engineer.

Vincent van Gogh - Vincent Willem van Gogh (1853–1890) was a Dutch Post-Impressionist artist. Most of his best-known works were produced in the final two years of his life, during which time he cut off part of his left ear following a breakdown in his friendship with Paul Gauguin. After this he suffered recurrent bouts of mental illness, and committed suicide.

CARAVAGGIO - Michelangelo Merisi da Caravaggio (1571 – 1610) was an Italian artist active in Rome, Naples, Malta and Sicily between 1593 and 1610. He is commonly placed in the Baroque school, of which he was the first great representative.

SALOME - The story of Salome is told in the New Testament: her stepfather, Herod Antipas, asked her to dance for him at a banquet and promised her anything she asked for in return. Prompted by her mother, Herodias, who had been angered that St. John the Baptist had criticized her marriage, Salome asked for the head of St. John, which was brought to her on a platter.

CALIGULA - Gaius Julius Caesar Augustus Germanicus (12 – 41), more commonly known by his nickname Caligula, was the third Roman Emperor. Known for his extreme extravagance, eccentricity, depravity and cruelty, he was assassinated by his own guards.

FRANGIPANI - Frangipani is the common name of Plumeria, a small genus of seven to eight plant species native to tropical and subtropical America. The plant produces flowers ranging from yellow to pink depending on form or cultivar.

BACALAO - *Bacalhau* means codfish in Portuguese, but the word almost always refers to salt cod and the dishes made from it. In Spanish speaking countries the dried fish and its resulting dishes are called *bacalao,*

FREDERIC REMINGTON - Frederic Remington (1861 - 1909) was an American painter, illustrator, sculptor, and writer who specialized in depictions of the American West. He was born in Canton, New York.

JOHN SINGER SARGENT - John Singer Sargent (1856 – 1925) was the most successful portrait painter of his era, as well as a gifted landscape painter and watercolorist. Sargent was born in Florence, Italy to American parents.

NICOLA D'INVERNO - An Italian model, d'Inverno was John Singer Sargent's valet from the early 1890s until 1918 and was rumored to be his lover.

CAMILLE PISSARRO - Camille Pissarro (1830 – 1903) was a French Impressionist painter. who was born in Charlotte Amalie, St. Thomas, Virgin Islands. Pissarro lived in St. Thomas until age twelve, when he went to a boarding school in Paris.

The author lived in St. Thomas. The poem was inspired by a sketch by Pissarro that appeared in the *New York Times*.

EUCHRE - Euchre is a trick-taking card game most commonly played with four people in partnership using a standard deck of twenty-four playing cards.

About the Author

Maurice Kenny was born in Watertown, New York in 1929. He was educated at Butler University, St. Lawrence University and New York University, where he studied with the eminent American poet, Louise Bogan. In the 1950s he took up residence in New York City for several years. In the early to mid-60s he lived in Mexico and the Virgin Islands, moving to Chicago for one year. From Chicago he moved to Brooklyn where he lived until his return to the Adirondack country of upstate New York.

He has been the co-editor of the literary review magazine *Contact/II* as well as the editor/publisher of Strawberry Press. He has also been poetry editor of *Adirondac Magazine*, Poet-in-Residence at North Country Community College, and Visiting Professor at the University of Oklahoma at Norman, Oklahoma, the En'owkin Center at the University of Victoria, in British Columbia and at Paul Smith's College. He is presently on the faculty of the SUNY College at Potsdam.

Kenny's work has been published in numerous journals, including *Trends, Calaloo, World Literature Today, American Indian Quarterly, Blue Cloud Quarterly, Wicazo Sa Review, Saturday* Review, and the *New York Times.*

In 2000, he received the Elder Recognition Award from the Wordcraft Circle of Native Writers. In 1996 *On Second Thought* was a finalist for the Oklahoma Book Award in fiction. *Blackrobe: Isaac Jogues,* was nominated for the Pulitzer Prize, as was *Between Two Rivers.* He is the recipient of a National Public Radio Award for Broadcasting. *The Mama Poems* received the American Book Award in 1984. The *Bloomsbury Review* cited *Wounds Beneath the Flesh,* which he edited, as the best anthology of 1983.

Kenny was honored with an honorary doctorate by St. Lawrence University in 1995. He presently divides his time between Saranac Lake and Potsdam, New York.